CIVILIZATIONS OF THE WORLD

AZTEC CIVILIZATION

by Tracy Vonder Brink

FOCUS READERS

NAVIGATOR

WWW.FOCUSREADERS.COM

Focus Readers is distributed by North Star Editions:
sales@northstareditions.com | 888-417-0195

Produced for Focus Readers by Red Line Editorial.

Content Consultant: Dr. Kirby Farah, Department of Anthropology, University of Southern California

Photographs ©: Millionstock/Shutterstock Images, cover, 1; David Hiser/National Geographic Image Collection/Alamy, 4–5; Fabio Imhoff/Shutterstock Images, 7, 27; Red Line Editorial, 8; Kiev.Victor/Shutterstock Images, 10–11; jos macouzet/Shutterstock Images, 13; Antwon McMullen/Shutterstock Images, 14; De Agostini Picture Library/De Agostini/Getty Images, 16–17; Eduardo Verdugo/AP Images, 19; Mireille Vautier/Alamy, 20; Itamar Japa Blog DMEC/Shutterstock Images, 22–23; Agatha Kadar/Shutterstock Images, 25; Mario Arturo Martinez/Agencia El Universal/EVZ/GDA/AP Images, 29

Library of Congress Cataloging-in-Publication Data
Names: Vonder Brink, Tracy, author.
Title: Aztec civilization / by Tracy Vonder Brink.
Description: Lake Elmo, MN : Focus Readers, 2020. | Series: Civilizations of the world | Audience: Grades 4 to 6. | Includes bibliographical references and index.
Identifiers: LCCN 2018060598 (print) | LCCN 2018061390 (ebook) | ISBN 9781641859646 (PDF) | ISBN 9781641858953 (ebook) | ISBN 9781641857574 (hardcover) | ISBN 9781641858267 (pbk.)
Subjects: LCSH: Aztecs--Juvenile literature.
Classification: LCC F1219.73 (ebook) | LCC F1219.73 .V66 2020 (print) | DDC 972--dc23
LC record available at https://lccn.loc.gov/2018060598

Printed in the United States of America
Mankato, MN
May, 2019

ABOUT THE AUTHOR

Tracy Vonder Brink loves true stories and has written dozens of articles for young readers. Many years ago, she visited Aztec ruins in Mexico, and the Aztec section is her favorite part of any museum. She lives in Ohio with her husband, two daughters, and two dogs.

TABLE OF CONTENTS

CHAPTER 1

A MULTI-ETHNIC EMPIRE

More than 500 years ago, one **empire** covered much of Mesoamerica. Mesoamerica is the name for a region covering parts of what is now Mexico and Central America. Today, the empire's people are known as the Aztecs. But the empire was actually made up of several different tribes.

Santa Cecilia Acatitlan is a restored Aztec temple that stands near Mexico City.

One tribe, the Mexica, conquered and ruled the others. The Mexica most likely came from the northern part of Mexico. Around the year 1325, they moved south. They settled in central Mexico. In this area, they built their capital city. It stood on an island in the middle of a lake.

Over the years, the capital city grew larger and more powerful. Its warriors invaded neighboring cities, where tribes such as the Mixtecs and Zapotecs lived. Each captured city had to pay a **tribute**. Rulers collected tributes at least once a year. Some cities gave gold or food. Others gave cloth or animal skins. The payments helped the empire prosper.

Ruins of Templo Mayor, the main temple of the Aztecs' capital city, are surrounded by Mexico City today.

Farming also helped the empire grow. Its people were skilled farmers. Builders dug waterworks. These structures carried river water to fields. In cities near lakes, farmers dug soil from lake bottoms. They piled up the soil to make small islands.

Farmers planted crops on the islands. They grew gardens in the middle of the lake. In this way, they had more land for growing food.

By 1519, the Aztec Empire had reached its peak. The empire included more than

THE AZTEC EMPIRE IN 1519

400 **city-states**. Between five and six million people lived under Aztec rule in these cities and the countryside around them. Soon, however, explorers from Spain arrived. These newcomers also wanted to control the land. Life for the Aztecs was about to change.

THE "AZTECS"

The people of central Mexico are often called Aztecs. But they didn't use this name themselves. Instead, the name likely came from a German explorer. He based the name on Aztlán, the region where the people originally came from. However, these people called themselves the Mexica. They called their capital city Tenochtitlán. The country of Mexico likely gets its name from this group of people.

CHAPTER 2

CITIES AND LEADERS

The Aztec Empire was made up of city-states. Several smaller groups, known as calpulli, joined together to form each city-state. A calpulli was a group of families. They lived together in one area of the city. A **noble** led each of these areas. Together, a city's nobles met to elect its leader, or *tlatoani*.

Cuauhtémoc was the last Aztec *tlatoani*. He ruled the capital city from 1520 to 1521.

Every city-state had its own leader. But the capital city was the most important. As a result, its leader had the most power. He was known as the *huey tlatoani*. Leaders of other city-states had to obey him. They also had to send him tributes.

Religion was a key part of life in the Aztec Empire. Most cities had at least one large stone pyramid. A temple stood on top of the pyramid. Smaller temples dotted the city streets. And every home had a **shrine**.

The Aztecs believed in hundreds of gods. They thought these gods controlled all parts of life. Many gods were based on things from the natural world, such as the

A statue of Tlaloc, the Aztec god of rain, stands in Mexico City.

sun, wind, or rain. Others were gods of healing or war.

Pleasing the gods was very important. The Aztecs believed terrible things would happen if the gods were unhappy. For example, an angry rain god might cause a drought. Then farmers' crops would die.

Carvings of skulls decorate a wall of the Templo Mayor complex.

To keep the gods happy, the Aztecs made **sacrifices**. Human life was the most valuable sacrifice. The sacrifices took place at the temples. Priests were in charge of carrying them out. Exactly how many people the Aztecs sacrificed is not known. But in 2015, hundreds of skulls were discovered below the spot where an Aztec temple once stood.

However, making sacrifices was not the only way the Aztecs tried to please the gods. They did other things, too. People sang songs they thought the gods liked to hear. They decorated shrines with flowers. And every month, they held celebrations to honor the gods. People danced and had parades.

AZTEC PRIESTS

Both men and women could become priests. To learn to be priests, children studied at special schools. They began attending these schools between the ages of 6 and 13. Besides making sacrifices, priests helped plan religious events. They even helped leaders decide the best days to go to war.

CHAPTER 3

DAILY LIFE

People in the Aztec Empire were divided into classes. Most people belonged to the bottom class. Members of this group were farmers. Their lives were full of hard work. They often rose at dawn and spent all day in the fields.

Farmers grew corn, tomatoes, beans, and squash. They lived in small houses.

This illustration shows the inside of an Aztec country home.

Most homes had a kitchen and one room for sleeping. As many as 12 people might live in one house. Farmers used **adobe** bricks to build their houses.

The middle class included craftsmen, merchants, and warriors. Craftsmen made pottery, jewelry, and other fine objects. Merchants sold and traded goods. They ran shops in the city's markets. Some merchants grew rich.

Warriors had a key role in Aztec life. They helped rulers conquer more people. When they won battles, they collected tributes and took prisoners. Often, these prisoners would be sacrificed. Successful warriors could become rich and famous.

A man in traditional clothing makes music with a seashell during a 2009 ceremony honoring Aztec history.

A small group of nobles and priests made up the top class. They were respected and wealthy. Many dressed in colorful clothes. They ate foods, such as chocolate, that other people weren't allowed to have. Nobles lived in stone palaces. Their homes had many rooms.

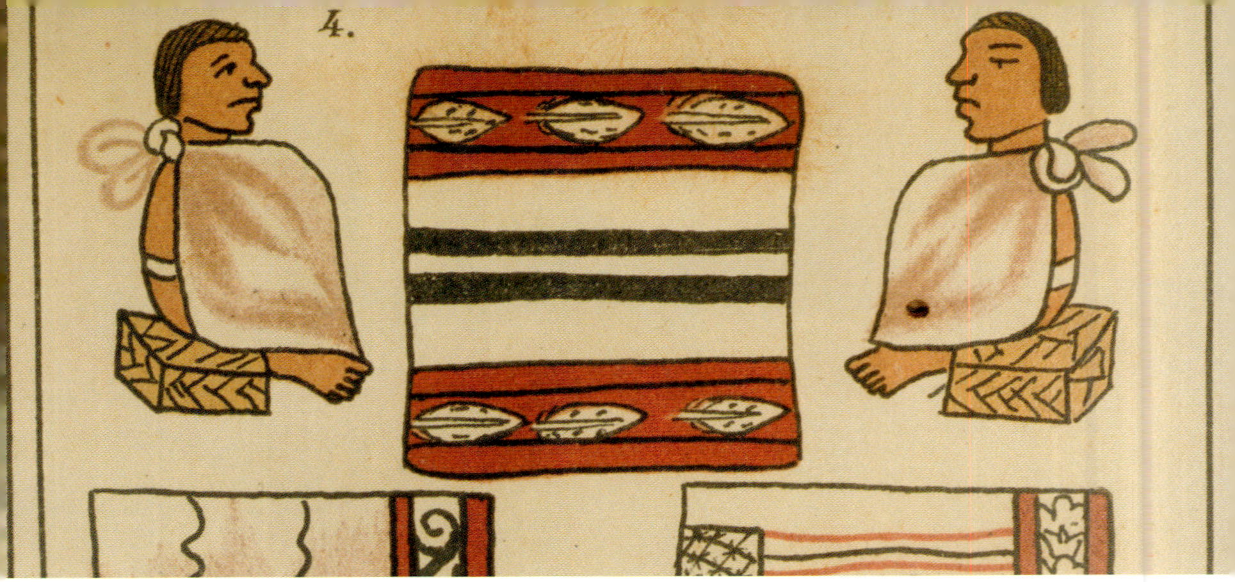

This illustration from the 1500s shows cloth and clothing made in the capital city of Tenochtitlán.

Some nobles worked for the government. Others led groups of warriors.

All Aztec children went to school. Some schools taught boys how to be farmers. Other schools trained boys to be warriors or priests. Some girls also studied to become priests or healers. However, weaving was the most important skill for girls to learn. Cloth was a valuable tribute. Only women wove cloth. So, they had a key role in the empire's economy.

Girls also learned to cook. Aztecs ate corn with most meals. They used it to make tortillas. Spicy peppers flavored their food. They also made popcorn for snacking.

PLAYING GAMES

Some Aztec cities had ball courts. Players scored points by knocking a hard rubber ball through a stone ring. They could use only their elbows, knees, or hips. Many people went to the ball courts to watch the teams play. Aztecs also played a board game called *patolli*. The board was shaped like an X. Players used beans or corn as pieces.

CHAPTER 4

RISE AND FALL

When the Mexica built their capital city in 1325, eight other city-states already existed nearby. People from these different tribes often lived and worked together. In 1428, Mexica leader Itzcóatl teamed up with two other city-states to form the Triple Alliance. The cities agreed to work together and help one another.

Teotihuacan was one of several great cities built before the Aztec Empire united Mesoamerica.

Together, warriors from the three cities won many battles. They conquered much of central and southern Mexico. Over the years, the Mexica's city-state became the center of a large empire. This empire included many different groups of people. Some were unhappy with the empire's rulers. Many tribes did not want to pay tributes.

In 1519, Motecuhzoma II led the empire's capital city. One day, he heard that strangers had landed on the coast. Motecuhzoma sent some of his men to meet them. The strangers said they were from Spain. They had come to explore the land and search for gold.

This feathered headdress may have been worn by Motecuhzoma II.

The Spanish leader, Hernán Cortés, wanted to meet Motecuhzoma. Cortés and his soldiers marched toward the empire's capital city. They visited other city-states along the way. Some city-states asked Cortés to fight the Aztec leaders. They promised to help Cortés if he did.

Motecuhzoma treated Cortés and his men as guests. But Cortés wanted to rule the Aztec Empire. Just a week later, he took Motecuhzoma prisoner. Fighting broke out between the two groups. Motecuhzoma was killed.

The Aztecs outnumbered the Spanish. But the Aztecs' wooden clubs and arrows were no match for swords and guns. The Spanish also brought diseases from Europe. Many Aztecs became ill and died. Losing so many warriors and leaders weakened the empire. In addition, some city-states joined the Spanish in fighting against the Aztecs. By 1521, the capital city had been destroyed.

Aztec priests wrote the Codex Borbonicus, a book about their religion, around the time the Spanish invaded.

When the Aztec Empire collapsed, life for the people of Mesoamerica changed. The Spanish took over the region. They attacked or enslaved the native tribes. Still, the tribes wrote about their history. They also left **artifacts**. Historians study these objects. They learn about life before the Spanish came to Mesoamerica. They study each tribe's customs and culture.

A BETTER RED

Wealthy Aztecs often wore bright-red clothing. The Spanish were surprised when they saw this color. In much of the world, red dye was made from plants. The dye was difficult to create. And its color was not very bright.

The Aztecs made their vibrant dye from an insect called the cochineal. This insect lives in prickly pear cactuses. It contains a chemical that tastes bad to predators. The chemical also makes a strong red color. The Aztecs collected the insects and dried their shells. Then they crushed the shells and boiled them in water. Depending on the process workers used, the shells could produce red, purple, or pink colors.

In the 1500s, Spanish merchants began shipping cochineal shells back to Europe. They sold huge amounts of the dye. Soon the rest of the

Grinding the shells of cochineal insects produces a bright-red dye.

world was using the Aztecs' method to make red dye. In fact, cochineal dye is still used today. It creates the color of many red lipsticks.

FOCUS ON

AZTEC CIVILIZATION

Write your answers on a separate piece of paper.

1. Write a sentence that summarizes the key ideas in Chapter 1.
2. Do you think farmers or warriors played a bigger role in the Aztecs' rise to power? Give two reasons to support your answer.
3. Which group of people was at the top of Aztec society?
   - **A.** farmers
   - **B.** priests
   - **C.** warriors
4. Why did other city-states ask the Spanish to fight the Aztecs?
   - **A.** They wanted the Aztecs to defeat the Spanish.
   - **B.** They were tired of living under Aztec rule.
   - **C.** They hoped the fighting would make the Spanish leave.

Answer key on page 32.

GLOSSARY

adobe
A mixture of mud and straw that is dried and hardened in the sun.

artifacts
Ancient objects made by humans.

city-states
Individual cities (and the areas around them) that have their own government and are not controlled by another country.

empire
A group of nations or territories ruled by a powerful government.

noble
A person of the highest social class.

sacrifices
Offerings or gifts given to please a god.

shrine
A place for religious worship, usually connected to a god, a holy person, or an event.

tribute
Something valuable that one group is forced to give to a more powerful group.

TO LEARN MORE

BOOKS

Farndon, John. *How to Live Like an Aztec Priest.* Minneapolis: Hungry Tomato, 2016.

Kenney, Karen Latchana. *Ancient Aztecs.* Minneapolis: Abdo Publishing, 2015.

Niver, Heather Moore. *Ancient Aztec Daily Life.* New York: PowerKids Press, 2017.

NOTE TO EDUCATORS

Visit **www.focusreaders.com** to find lesson plans, activities, links, and other resources related to this title.

INDEX

Answer Key: 1. Answers will vary; **2.** Answers will vary; **3.** B; **4.** B